MOSHKEL GOSHA

A STORY OF TRANSFORMATION

MOSHKEL GOSHA

A STORY OF TRANSFORMATION

A COMMENTARY *by* LLEWELLYN VAUGHAN-LEE

THE GOLDEN SUFI CENTER

First published in the United States in 2005 by
The Golden Sufi Center
P.O. Box 456, Point Reyes Station, California 94956
www.goldensufi.org

Printed in the USA.

Paperback ISBN 13: 978-1-941394-29-8
Hardcover ISBN 13: 978-1-890350-10-9

Library of Congress Cataloging-in-Publication Data
Vaughan-Lee, Llewellyn.
  Moshkel Gosha, a story of transformation :
a commentary / by Llewellyn Vaughan-Lee.
      p. cm.
  Includes bibliographical references.
ISBN 1-941394-29-8
 1. Mushkil Gushâ (Tale)--History and criticism.
 2. Sufi parables--Iran. I. Title.
 GR75.M92V38 2005
 398.2'0955'02--dc22
                              2004060685

CONTENTS

INTRODUCTION

HE story of Moshkel Gosha is an ancient Persian story. Told in many different versions, it was as well-known in Persia as Cinderella is in Europe. The story of Moshkel Gosha also belongs to the Sufi tradition. It has a particular association with Bahâ ad-dîn Naqshband (1318-1389), who gave his name to the Naqshbandi Order of Sufism. It is found in a well-known story about Bahâ ad-dîn's birth:

> A Sufi Master, Khwâja Babâ Samâsî, was passing through a village later known as Arifan, when he said to his companions: "This soil smells of a hero." Passing again soon after he said: "The smell is stronger, be sure that the hero is born." In fact, three days previously Bahâ ad-dîn came into the world.
>
> A while later, the child's grandfather, according to the custom of the time, placed a gift on Bahâ ad-dîn's

heart, and asked Babâ Samâsî to bless him. The Khwâja said: "This is the hero whose smell we were aware of. Before long the aroma will spread through the world and he will become the *moshkel gosha* of the people of love.[1]

Moshkel Gosha means in Persian literally "the remover of obstacles," and the story is about allowing the transpersonal, or spiritual, dimension to enter into our lives, and so to bring about a process of transformation. However, this story suggests that this dimension, this wealth which lies within us, is not so easy to recognise, nor do we necessarily know how to put it to its proper use. "Moshkel Gosha" also concerns the danger of inflation, a danger which is always present when working with the transpersonal, particularly if the individual does not have sufficient humility. Thus "Moshkel Gosha" is a story which touches on some of the most important issues that relate to experiencing and integrating the potential that the inner world has to offer. Moreover, the story of Moshkel Gosha is not just about what happens to one bush-digger and his daughter, but it is the story of anyone who receives help from within, whether through dreams, meditation, or any other way by which the transpersonal is able to enter into our lives. One woman, after hearing the story of Moshkel Gosha, was very moved, but felt she didn't really understand its message. The next morning she heard a voice telling her to go to a small chapel nearby. At first she didn't listen to the voice, but then she went to the chapel, and found that it was full of vermilion light. She thought, "This light can't be for me." In that moment the light vanished, and then she understood the story of Moshkel Gosha.

In its essence, "Moshkel Gosha" is the story of our own individual relationship with the inner world. And because we are living at a time when there is great need to realize the healing power that lies within us, this story should not be forgotten, for, in the words of Moshkel Gosha, when it is told, "the people who are in real need will be able to find their way."

THE STORY
OF
MOSHKEL GOSHA

ONCE upon a time there was a Baba Kharkan, a prickly-bush digger, who lived with his wife and daughter in a very small house outside the town. Each day he would go out to dig prickly bushes in order to take them to town and sell them for firewood. With the proceeds he would buy simple food for his wife and daughter. They always had enough to eat, and remained thankful to God.

However, there came a day when his daughter complained to him that she was fed up with always eating such plain food. She asked "Why can't we be like some of the townsfolk and have different foods to eat?" So persistent was she that the poor man decided to try and please her. That day he went far out into the scrub-land to find more wood than usual. He dug up a large number of bushes and brought them back, but when he returned, it was already quite dark, and there was no light in his house. His wife and daughter thought that he was spending the night in town, and had gone to sleep. They were both heavy sleepers and were not awakened by his knocking. Unable to enter his own house, the bush-digger lay down on the ground outside, and, because he was so tired, he soon fell fast asleep.

But the ground was hard and cold, and with the first dew in the early hours the bush-digger awoke. Again he knocked on the door of his house, and again there was no answer. By this time he was both cold and hungry, but he decided to go very early to work. This time he went even further, and found more wood than before, but because he had gone so far out into the scrub-land, it was again late when he returned. Once again the two women were fast asleep, and did not respond to his knocking. His wife and daughter had been worried about him, but presumed that he had met some friends in town and stayed with them. This had happened a few times before, so they had eaten their simple supper and gone to bed.

Tired and even hungrier, the bush-digger lay down on the cold ground. Just as he was falling asleep, he thought he heard a voice that said: "Wake up! Leave your bundle of bushes and come this way. If you need enough and want little enough, you shall find wonderful food."

So the bush-digger got up and followed the direction of the voice into the darkness. But there was nothing there, and so dark was the night that he realized he could not find his way back to his house. Now not only was he tired and hungry, but he was lost. He lay down on the ground feeling miserable and tried to sleep. But he was too miserable to sleep. So he looked back over everything that had happened to him since his daughter had asked for something more than their simple diet. As if telling himself a story, he told himself the events of the last two days.

The moment he had finished telling himself this story, he thought he heard another voice. This voice, which seemed to come from above, asked him why he was so miserable. Once again the bush-digger told his story. Then the voice told him to close his eyes and climb up a step. "What step?" asked the poor man, "I cannot see any step." "Just do as you are told," the voice answered.

So the man closed his eyes and climbed this imaginary step. It felt very real, and then there was another step and another. The man found that he could climb very easily, and he went up and up. Then the steps ended and the voice said, "Now you can open your eyes." The bush-digger opened his eyes and saw that he was in a great desert. The sun beat down from above, and around him, on the ground, were many different-colored pebbles which glistened in the sunshine.

Once again the voice spoke to him: "Pick up as many of these stones as you can. Then close your eyes and go back down the steps."

The man looked around to see where the voice came from. He could see nobody there. But he did as he was told. He filled his pockets with stones, closed his eyes, and went down the invisible steps. When he came to the bottom of the steps he opened his eyes and found that he was in front of his own house. Day was breaking and he heard from inside the house the sounds of his wife and daughter getting up. He knocked on the door, and his daughter opened it. He went inside, and they shared some dried fruit together as he told them what had happened. He emptied his pockets on the table and the stones he had picked up from the desert rolled out, to the astonishment of his wife and daughter.

When they had all finished their simple breakfast, once again the bush-digger heard a voice speaking to him. Only he could hear the voice, but it spoke very clearly to him, "What has happened to you has been through the grace of Moshkel Gosha. You must remember that Moshkel Gosha is always present, even if you do not realize it. Each Thursday you must eat some dried fruit, and give some to someone in need. Then you must tell the story of Moshkel Gosha. If you do this, the story of Moshkel Gosha will always be remembered, and those who are in real need will be able to find their way."

The man then put the stones away in a corner near the stove. They looked very ordinary, and he did not know what to do with them. Then he carried all the wood he had collected into the town, where he sold it for a good price. As well as their staple food, he bought his wife and daughter some delicacies that he knew they would like, and returned home. That evening they had a delicious meal together.

So the life of the prickly-bush digger appeared to return to normal. He went out each day to dig prickly bushes, which he took to the town to sell. However, he always found big bushes that dug up easily, and so was able to buy a few different types of food.

However, when next Thursday came, he had forgotten all about Moshkel Gosha. During the evening his nearest neighbor who lived half a mile distant knocked on the door. His fire had gone out, and he had come to ask for a couple of hot coals. When the bush-digger opened the door, the neighbor said, "Can I borrow one of your coals that are glowing so brightly? I could see the light through the window as I was walking here."

Looking in through his own window, the bush-digger saw that the stones he had left by the stove were glowing brightly. But when he went to where they were, he found that their light was cold and could not light a fire. He returned to his neighbor and said, "I am afraid that you are mistaken. I don't have any coals." And he shut the door in his neighbor's face and then also closed the shutters on the window.

Together with his wife and daughter, he went again to look at the stones, and discovered that they were precious jewels. "Now we have a real reason to celebrate," he said, "bit by bit I can take these stones to the neighboring towns and sell them. Then we can build ourselves a palace and live like kings." And this is precisely what they did.

Then, one day, it so happened that the king, accompanied by his viziers, was going back to his palace after a day of hunting. By chance he passed the lofty new palace built by the bush-digger, and, being extremely surprised, he inquired about the owner. His courtiers informed him that it had been built quite recently, and that no one knew who owned it. All anyone knew was that the owner's name was La 'l-e Sowdagar (gem trader). Hearing this the king consulted with his left-hand and right-hand viziers. One of them suggested they go to the palace and, under the pretext of getting some water for the king, try to find out what was going on and who owned it. Everyone agreed and so they approached the palace, and when someone came to the door, one of the courtiers said, "His Imperial Majesty, the Center of the Universe, is returning to his palace from hunting and is thirsty. We wish to have some water."

It so happened that the bush-digger himself answered the door; so, having heard the request, he bowed, saying, "But of course, by all means; it is a pleasure." He then rushed in and filled a gold and jewel-studded cup with cardamom and rosewater sherbet and handed it over to the king. After drinking the sherbet the king looked at the cup and said, "What a beautiful cup. There is nothing like it in my entire treasury."

The prickly-bush digger bowed once more and said, "May I present it to Your Majesty?" The king was pleased. He then asked who owned the palace. The bush-digger answered, "Your Majesty, it belongs to your servant and slave, La 'l-e Sowdagar." The king headed home without waiting any longer. On his arrival he ran to his daughter who inquired why he was back so early. The king told her the entire story. Having no playmate, the princess said, "I wish you had asked him whether he had a daughter about my age, so she could be my lady-in-waiting." The king immediately sent some of his servants to inquire. On their return they reported that not only had La 'l-e Sowdagar a daughter, but she was so beautiful that she called on the moon not to come up, for she could illumine the night by herself. They concluded that she was perfect to become the princess's lady-in-waiting.

The princess dispatched her servants to bring her over. The bush-digger's daughter was delighted and started for the king's palace. At first the princess felt jealous of the girl's beauty, but soon they became fast friends. They met every day, and would often go and swim and play in a stream that the king had made for his daughter. One day, the princess was wearing a beautiful necklace, and before she went bathing, she took it off and hung it on a tree beside the stream. When she had got out of the water she forgot that she had hung it on the tree, and not being able to find it, she decided that her new lady-in-waiting had stolen it.

The princess told this to her father, who had the girl, her mother, and her father arrested. The two women were sold into slavery, and the man was sent to prison. The curious thing, however, was that when the soldiers went to confiscate La 'l-e Sowdagar's palace and furniture they found that everything had turned to smoke and disappeared.

The bush-digger's new-found wealth had come to a sorry end. He was treated like a common criminal. No more sherbet or delicate meats for his meals. He had to live off bread and water and sleep on dirty straw. Then one Wednesday night he had a dream: A luminous holy man, wearing green slippers, cloak, and turban, approached him and, touching him with his walking stick, said, "O you inwardly blind, you have forgotten to remember Moshkel Gosha. Now, get up; there is a penny hidden under the doorsill. Take it, buy some dried fruit, and fulfill your vow."

The man woke up with a start, and then remembered his dream. At the same time he realized that it was now Thursday. He searched for the penny and sure enough there it was. He picked up the money and called through the keyhole to the jailer, saying, "God bless you, brother, please take this coin and buy me some dried fruit." The guard said, "I must say, you have some nerve. You want me to go on a silly errand so that you can escape. No, nothing doing."

A couple of minutes later the bush-digger repeated the same request to a man on a horse he saw passing by outside the jail window, but the man made some excuse and went on his way. Then he noticed an old woman slowly walking by. The man appealed to her, "God bless you, lady. Please take this penny and get me some dried fruit so that I can fulfill my vow."

The old woman replied, "Dear sir, my son is dying, but never mind, I will help you." So the old woman brought the fruit, and the bush-digger thanked her and asked her if she would share it with him and just listen to his story. She consented, and just as he finished telling his story someone rushed by and called out to the old woman, "You may not believe this, but your son has just managed to escape from the claws of Azra'il, the angel of death! He is calling for you."

Now, that day, the princess happened to go again to bathe in the stream. She thought she saw her necklace lying on the bottom of the stream. But as she looked again she realized it was a reflection of her necklace that she saw. She looked up, and there, still hanging on the branch where she had left it, was her necklace. She rushed to the king and told him the news. The king then ordered the bush-digger and his family to be freed.

Afterwards the princess and the girl became friends again, and strangely enough, when the prickly-bush digger and his wife went back to their home, they saw that their palace was still there. So once again the prickly-bush digger became La 'l-e Sowdagar, and they all lived happily ever after.

We beseech God to fulfill your wish as He fulfilled theirs. God willing.

THE COMMENTARY

HE story of Moshkel Gosha is a tale of transformation. It speaks of how a human being can awaken to the dimension of the soul and help the energies of the inner worlds nourish outer life. Like the fairy tales of Europe, it reflects the magic and dangers of a relationship with archetypal energies. Because it follows the twists and turns of one man's awakening, it is alive with the potential to awaken others. This is one of the great gifts of such a story—it is always alive. The story itself contains and reflects the energies of inner dimensions, which can nourish those who truly listen. And in today's world, many of us are like the bush-digger's daughter, in need of a new form of nourishment, hungry for sustenance beyond the goods of our material culture. Listening to the tale of Moshkel Gosha, the remover of obstacles, invites Moshkel Gosha into our lives, and helps him clear away that which stands between us and the wonders of the soul.

1
THE NEEDS OF THE SOUL

HE story of Moskel Gosha is about Baba Kharkan, a prickly-bush digger, and his daughter. A prickly-bush digger is a Persian equivalent to the woodcutter—a frequent figure in European folk tales. Both represent honest, simple folk, who live and work in the natural world. In contrast to the civilized environment of the town, or the cultivated landscape of the farmer, the bush-digger works in the uncultivated scrubland, a world belonging solely to the forces of nature. He images the part of our own, ordinary self that is open to our inner nature and able to be touched by its transformative qualities.

The bush-digger lives outside the town with his wife and daughter. He makes a simple living by selling his wood in the town, and they always have enough to eat. But there comes a time when his daughter is no longer satisfied with their simple diet, and she demands different kinds of food. The bush-digger's daughter can be understood as his anima or soul-figure.

Thus his soul-figure demands to be nurtured in a different way; the food given by the ordinary experiences of life is no longer sufficient.

The demand by the inner self for a new form of nourishment can manifest in people's lives in many different ways. It can surface as a discontent with one's present job or relationship, a desire to be more creative, or even the need to follow a spiritual path. And people respond to this call in a variety of ways. In this story, the response of the bush-digger is to go further out into the scrub-land and find more wood, which he can then sell and thus be able to buy his daughter what she wants. And yet, when he returns after a day of work, he finds the door of his house locked against him. His wife and daughter are asleep and do not answer to his knocking.

Why does this happen to the hardworking bush-digger? What is amiss with his plan? It would seem that his response to his daughter's request is very rational, and possibly this is the problem. For when the inner self requests more nourishment, to offer merely more of the same form of nourishment is not the answer.

The inner self is asking for a different quality, not quantity, of nourishment. For example, if one works hard and accumulates material wealth and then feels an inner discontent, to work harder and accumulate more will not help. The inner self needs a different quality of life. Maybe it is time to look to the inner life rather than the outer, to be more creative or reflective. The bush-digger's response was not appropriate; thus he finds himself locked out of his house.

The bush-digger knocks on his door three times before events begin to change and he encounters Moshkel Gosha. There is an esoteric tradition that if you knock three times, the door must be opened; if you ask a question three times, it must be answered. A well-known example of this is in the *Katha Upanishad* when the boy Nachiketas meets the Spirit of Death and three times asks to be told the truth about death before he is answered. The bush-digger knocks three times, and another world is opened to him.

First, the bush-digger hears a voice saying: "Wake up! Leave your bundle of bushes and come this way. If you need enough and want little enough, you shall find wonderful food." The first step for the bush-digger is to leave his wood, which represents his own conditioned approach to supporting and nourishing himself and his daughter. Before anyone can enter into the inner world and be given a different form of nourishment, whether in a psychological or a spiritual sense, he must "wake up" and leave behind his conditioned approach, often the values of the outer world.

But the second half of the voice's statement, comparing need and want, is also profound. For in the process of inner transformation, the discrimination between "need" and "want" is of utmost importance. "Need" is what is necessary for our life. It can refer to the physical need for food, clothing, shelter, etc., or it can be an inner need, for love, security, understanding, etc. It can also be a need of the soul, for creativity or spiritual nourishment. However, "want" always refers to the desires of the ego, which do not have to be fulfilled. In fact, the desires of the ego often deafen an individual to the call of his true needs, especially when these are needs of the soul, which may take him beyond the realm of the ego.

But the voice not only differentiates between "need" and "want," it also says the "need" must be "enough." One's inner need, the need of the soul, is only answered if it is great enough, for then the human being calls out in such a way that the call must be answered: answered essentially by the higher Self. This is the value of despair, for when one reaches a point of total despair then one calls out in great need, and such a call is always answered. But here lies the significance of the voice's second condition, to "want little enough." For while the answer is always there, once again the demands of the ego can be so loud that one does not hear it.

The need of the soul is like an empty cup waiting, indeed longing, to be filled. The need must be great, and yet the seeker should not want anything, for the cup is always filled through the grace of God in whom we must put our total trust. To want something is to condition or define the response, and how can we define the response of God? How can the ego know either the need of the soul or how God might respond? To want something is to cover the cup with our desires and conditioning, to put our ego before God. Thus the correct attitude, according to the Sufi saint

Moshkel Gosha

in Irina Tweedie's *Daughter of Fire*, is that of
the devotee:

> "If you ask the devotee what he wants,
> he will answer: nothing!"[2]

2
THE STEP INTO THE UNKNOWN

HE bush-digger "followed the direction of the voice into the darkness, but there was nothing there...." And now, not only is he tired and hungry, but he is "lost." How often before we find, or are shown, a new direction do we come to a place in ourself and our life where we feel totally lost. We do not know where to go or what to do. Like the bush-digger we are tired and exhausted and there seems nothing in our life, in our job or relationships, to sustain us.

This is what has happened to our bush-digger. Lying on the ground, unable to sleep, he tells himself the story of "everything that had happened to him since his daughter had asked for something more than their simple diet," and it is in telling this story that he is finally answered.

The telling of a story has great mythic significance; it is as if through the simple act of telling one's tale the magical doors to the inner world can open. Through the telling of one's story, something is made conscious; we are no longer completely caught in the play of events. A space is created, and into this space help can come. Telling one's story, either to oneself or a receptive listener, has a great healing quality, and it can open us to something beyond the ego.

The moment the bush-digger finishes telling himself his story, the voice speaks to him again, and asks him why he is so miserable. Again the poor man tells his story, and the voice tells him to close his eyes and climb a step. When the bush-digger says that he doesn't see any step, he is answered, "Just do as you are told."

The first step is always a step into the dark and must be an act of faith. Furthermore, the bush-digger is even told to close his eyes, for he has to make the transition from the outer world of the senses into the inner, imaginal world of the soul. The bush-digger does as he is told and finds the steps into the inner world easy to climb.

When the bush-digger finally opens his eyes, he finds himself in another world, a desert with the sun beating down on him. He has been taken into the inner world of the soul, which appears as a desert because it is a transcendent dimension, a place of revelation. The desert traditionally symbolizes the most propitious place for divine revelation. "This is because the desert, in so far as it is in a way a negative landscape, is outside the sphere of existence, susceptible only to things transcendent. Furthermore, the desert is the domain of the sun, not as the creator of energy upon earth but as pure celestial radiance, blinding in its manifestation."[3]

In the desert, with the sun beating down, the bush-digger finds masses of pebbles. When we are taken, through need and grace, into the inner world, we find something both most ordinary and of great value, our real Self. In the inner world the qualities of our true being are plentiful—they are just lying around on the ground. They are part of the substance of our being, the real ground on which we walk. The fact that the pebbles are many and of different colors expresses the many and varied manifestations of the Self, for, "smaller than small, greater than great," the Self can be seen as both One and many:

> That, many-formed, sustains the
>   whole earth,
> That, uniting, becomes One only.[4]

The voice then tells him, "Pick up as many of these stones as you can. Then close your eyes and go back down the steps." What does it mean to take these stones from the imaginal world down into the ordinary world? For when the bush-digger opens his eyes he finds himself "in front of his own house." Carl Jung, whose work has helped us to understand the dynamics of the symbolic world, continually asserts that these images from within only have meaning if they are integrated into the ordinary life of the individual, if they are "lived." If an archetypal symbol remains solely as an imaginal, inner experience, it has no value.

It is easy to be given a glimpse of the inner world, to experience that moment of grace when the veils lift and we are taken into the reality of the Self. In this moment everything is just as it should be, simple and profound, and we experience the oneness that is. We might taste a harmony, completeness, or love that is within us, or sense the infinite nature of our true being, its beauty and mystery. There are many ways the Self reveals itself to us. The work is always to bring this inner experience into the fabric of our everyday life, to live the Self not as a spiritual fantasy but as a grounded experience that nourishes us. The bush-digger must take home as many of the stones as he can; he must attempt to integrate as much of these numinous inner qualities, which symbolize his own wholeness, as he is able. It is this process of integration and the mistakes he makes in it that occupy the rest of the tale.

3
MOSHKEL GOSHA
AND THE
REMEMBRANCE
OF THE INNER WORLD

WHEN the bush-digger knocks this time on his door, it is, of course, opened by his daughter. Then he goes into the house and shares some dried fruit with his family as he tells them what has happened. The sharing of dried fruit forms an important part of the Persian ritual *Ajil-e Moshkel Gosha*, as it has been practiced for centuries and continues to be practiced today. Moshkel Gosha is the remover of obstacles, and so this ritual is performed by anyone who wishes to have a problem resolved.

The person performing this ritual ties some money, usually in coins, in the corner of a handkerchief and hands it over to the dried fruit seller. The shopkeeper or stallkeeper will then make up exactly the correct traditional combination of dried fruits and nuts. The shopkeeper passes this over to the customer, neither of whom utters a word during the course of the transaction. It should be noted that the *Ajil* (dried fruits and nuts) must be purchased from a shop facing Mecca. The ritual takes place either on the first or the last Thursday of each lunar month.

The *Ajil* is taken home and cleaned by several people. The inedible parts are always collected with care and thrown into a running stream. Then the fruit and nuts are laid out on a cloth in five piles, one at each corner and one in the center. Moshkel Gosha is remembered and in his name problems are discussed while the *Ajil* is shared with friends.[5] The symbolic significance of this ritualistic custom lies not only in the remembering of Moshkel Gosha, for the handkerchief and its five piles of *Ajil* form a mandala, a symbol of wholeness. The ritual helps bring forth wholeness through the resolution of psychological conflict.

Ajil comes from the Sufi tradition, for the original *Ajil*, and nuts in particular, are traditionally the only source of nourishment taken by Sufis going into retreat, which usually lasts for forty days. They consume nothing, it is said, but a single nut per day, thus depriving themselves of any other kind of food. At the end of forty days their wish, the object of their fast, will be granted. It is also said that at the end of the forty-day retreat Khidr, the archetypal figure of direct revelation,[6] appears to those who have successfully completed the period of the retreat and grants their wishes.

It is evident that *Ajil* symbolizes spiritual nourishment, and what is important in the story of Moshkel Gosha is that this nourishment be shared. At first the bush-digger shares the dried fruit with his wife and daughter and tells them his story. Then he hears the same voice that told him to climb the stairs:

> "What has happened to you has been through the grace of Moshkel Gosha. You must remember that Moshkel Gosha is always present, even if you do not realize it. Each Thursday you must eat some dried fruit, and give some to someone in need. Then you must tell the story of Moshkel Gosha. If you do this, the story of Moshkel Gosha will always be remembered, and those who are in real need will be able to find their way."

This is the first mention of Moshkel Gosha, the "remover of all difficulties." It is Moshkel

Gosha who has helped the bush-digger discover the nourishment of the inner worlds, and the man must "remember that Moshkel Gosha is always present." Remembrance not only functions as a mental recall, it is also an act of re-membering, or reconnecting an individual with that spiritual principle within, the wholeness that is our essential nature. For the Sufi the remembrance of God is a central spiritual practice, often combined with the repetition of a name of God in a *dhikr*.

For the bush-digger the act of remembrance is to be focused on Thursday, when he is to share some dried fruit and tell the story of Moshkel Gosha. Whilst Sunday is the Christian day of worship, Saturday the Jewish Sabbath, and Friday prayers the most important for the Muslim, the Sufi day is traditionally Thursday. Both Monday and Thursday were days of special fasting and spiritual observance for the Sufi, but over the course of time this became focused on Thursday. Thus the remembrance of Moshkel Gosha is firmly placed within a Sufi context.

The bush-digger is told to share some dried fruit with "someone in need" and tell the story of Moshkel Gosha. As our deepest needs are miraculously answered, we pass on this inner nourishment. It is a spiritual law that one is never given to for oneself, only for others:

> We are never given for ourselves, never; we are given for others. And the more you will give, the more you will receive; this is how the Essence works.[7]

The sharing of dried fruit symbolizes the sharing of spiritual or psychological suste-nance, similar to the loaves and fishes that Christ gave the multitude. But what is the significance of sharing a story? How can that help us?

Stories of the inner worlds have a great healing and transformative quality, as was known by our ancestors who ritually shared their myths. Through the telling of a mythic or archetypal story, the receptive listener is transported into the inner dimensions, where the soul can be directly nourished. Sadly, our contemporary culture has lost contact with this dimension of storytelling, and aside from our children's fairy tales, our stories themselves have lost their potency. They no longer evoke the archetypal world for the listener. The recent popularity of Harry Potter and Tolkien's *The Lord of the Rings* trilogy, though, suggests that our hunger for stories, which connect us with the magic of the inner worlds, is very present.

Just as we have lost touch with the power of storytelling in general, we have also forgotten the power of an individual telling his or her own tale. The archetypal world does not belong just to kings, witches, and princesses, but is within each of us; it makes its presence felt in our lives through dreams, visions, and synchronistic or magical events. The inner world is more present than our rational consciousness allows us to realize, but when we hear someone share such an experience, it awakens our own inner connection. We are no longer strangers exiled from ourself. This is one of the great benefits of dreamwork in a group; listening to another's dream brings alive our own dream world and the value and nourishment it has to offer us.

Telling our own story of the inner world is often more valuable than reciting from books or telling the stories of others. The symbols and images of the inner world carry a numinosity that can be transmitted in the telling. This numinosity is the dynamic energy of the inner world itself, for symbols, events, and archetypes are "living psychic forces." This energy, which is a magical power, has the potential to reach deep within the listener. Essentially, the symbols and events experienced by the teller can evoke themselves within a receptive listener, offering the possibility of a similar depth, or quality, of nourishment.

The story of Moshkel Gosha is the bush-digger's personal story of how one in real need receives help from within, and it is this which we should never, never forget. As we listen to such stories and remember the inner world, we remain open and receptive to inner guidance and nourishment, just as those who listen to the bush-digger's personal story are given their own access to the help of Moshkel Gosha.

The real danger lies in our forgetting this source of help, as is so evident in much of our present-day Western society, in which we have come to believe that help comes only from outside ourselves. Usually we look for it in the form of material assistance; we often place this burden on organizations or governments. But so long as we are aware of the guidance and nourishment that lie within, then "those who are in real need will be able to find their way."

4
THE COMMONEST THING

IN the story of Moshkel Gosha, the bush-digger puts the stones in a corner of his house, where "they looked very ordinary and he did not know what to do with them." Thus the story underscores the paradoxical nature of the Self. While our real Self is our greatest treasure, at the same time it is nothing special or spectacular. In the words of T. S. Eliot, our true nature is "a condition of complete simplicity." It is so ordinary that we easily overlook and dismiss it.

Alchemists refer to the Self as being like a *lapis*, or the philosopher's stone, "the commonest thing to be picked up anywhere," and they associated it with the Judeo-Christian metaphor of "the cornerstone which the builders rejected."[8] As Jung comments, the symbols of the Self have "an ordinary aspect [which is] not recognized by the worldly wise."[9]

How do we know what to do with this great treasure, our real Self? We are conditioned to believe that what is valuable is to be found in the outer world, in what we can possess. The symbols of the Self, the stones that the bush-digger finds, have a very different purpose than the goals and expectations of the ego. They belong to a dimension beyond our conscious self. While the Self embodies our essential human nature, its value and purpose cannot be appreciated from the perspective of the mind and our everyday values. This in itself makes a profound statement about what it really means to be a human being.

Leaving the stones in a corner of his little house, the bush-digger goes to market and sells all the wood he has collected, and with the money brings home for his daughter "all sorts of delicacies that he knew she would like." For the next week the bush-digger's life seemingly returns to normal.

And yet, though he has done nothing with the stones, the story hints that they already have a certain effect, in that he always finds "big bushes that dug up easily, and so was able to buy a few different types of food." Thus Moshkel Gosha continues to work in the bush-digger's life, silently and invisibly removing difficulties.

From a psychological perspective, the stones are symbols of wholeness he has brought into his ordinary, everyday life. Working silently within, the energy of the Self helps integrate conflicting aspects of the psyche and thus brings order and harmony into the life of the human being. As the individual is more integrated within himself, so this will be reflected in his external life, and previous difficulties will cease to exist.

However, because this process starts in the unconscious and slowly manifests from within, the conscious mind of the individual is often the last to notice any change. The danger is that since we are so conditioned to value only what is immediately visible we forget to value the slow process of transformation and inner nourishment.

This is what happens with the bush-digger. After the initial experience of the miraculous nature of the inner world, he slips back into unconsciousness, and when the next Thursday comes he has forgotten about Moshkel Gosha.

It is at this point that something happens to the stones lying in the corner of his hut. The fire in the house of the bush-digger's neighbor has gone out, and having nothing to re-light his fire, he goes to the house of

the bush-digger, where he sees brilliant lights
shining through the window. Presuming that
these lights come from coals, he asks for a light.
The bush-digger, going outside his house, also
sees the lights, which he discovers come from
the pile of pebbles. But the rays of light are
cold, and cannot light a fire, and so he shuts
the door in his neighbor's face.

5
THE INFLATION
OF THE BUSH-DIGGER

THE bush-digger forgets about Moshkel Gosha, but this gift is not for him alone. His neighbor comes to him to re-light his fire, symbolically alluding to the need for the transformative principle imaged in Moshkel Gosha. In response to this need the stones give out a light. They begin to reveal their true nature, their radiance.

But why is the light cold? If it is to be shared, why is it not ready for the neighbor to use? This coldness is significant, for while the energies of the inner dimensions can nourish us and our world, they require our own human participation. The human dimension gives warmth to the energies of the symbolic world.

The energies of the inner worlds are impersonal forces existing in the depths of the psyche. It is through our conscious relationship with them that their numinous energy can be integrated and used creatively. This is why, when we work with dreams or visions, it is always important to connect to the feeling-tone of the experience and understand what it means to us. This way we become a bridge so the inner can nourish our conscious life.

However, having slipped into forgetfulness, the bush-digger has no such relationship to his stones; he has left them in the corner, not knowing what to do with them. Thus, although the stones reveal their light, their numinosity, this energy is cold, and cannot be used to light the neighbor's fire.

Not only is the light from the stones cold, but so is the bush-digger's heart as he bangs the door in his neighbor's face and jealously hides his "treasure." Having forgotten Moshkel Gosha, the bush-digger's ego has taken over, and he now believes that the stones belong to him. This is essentially an attitude of inflation that can, as we shall see, have disastrous results.

When we make contact with the power and possibilities of the inner world, there is always the danger that the ego can identify with these energies and forget their transpersonal nature. In the worst case the ego is assimilated by the archetype and lives out its fate.[10] The bush-digger images the more ordinary danger of thinking that what is given from the inner world belongs to the ego: *I* have received inner wisdom, *I* have become a healer, *I* have become enlightened. The ego tries to subvert the inner world for its own power dynamics or sense of self-importance. We do not recognize that the experience belongs to a bigger dimension than our ego-self, which has to learn to be in service to what we have been given. Sadly, many people who have received gifts from the inner world have not made this step, and instead of real service exhibit a certain arrogance and coldness.

The bush-digger's fall begins because he has forgotten his obligations; he has forgotten to tell the story of Moshkel Gosha. Jung comments on the danger of forgetting one's ethical obligations to the energies of the unconscious:

> Not to do so [fulfill one's ethical obligations] is to fall prey to the power principle, and this produces dangerous effects which are destructive not only to others but even to the knower. The images of the unconscious place a great responsibility upon a man. Failure to

understand them, or a shirking of one's ethical responsibility, deprives him of his wholeness and imposes a painful fragmentation on his life.[11]

We do not realize how an inner experience places upon us a responsibility to the experience, to honor and live it as is needed. This is why, in many traditions, the individual is given access to the transpersonal world only after initiations that test his attitude and resolve. These traditions may have been lost; instead it is left to the individual to have the correct attitude to the inner world. But as many fairy tales warn us, we should never use the energy of the archetypal world for personal gain. This is what the bush-digger does.

For a short while the bush-digger enjoys the fruits of his actions. He sells the stones in neighboring towns for a huge price, and builds a wonderful palace for himself and his wife and daughter. This symbolically describes his state of inflation, in which he uses the energy of the unconscious for the power purposes of the ego. The worldly or ego-centered dimension of his attitude is imaged in his desire to "live like kings." The king is the ruler of this world, and it is in this direction that the bush-digger has focused his attention. He has forgotten Moshkel Gosha, the source of his new-found wealth.

6
THE KING
AND HIS DAUGHTER

THE story of Moshkel Gosha is an archetypal drama about accessing the dimension of the soul and using the energy of the inner worlds to nourish life. The details of the story highlight some underlying personal and collective dynamics that come to light as one lives the energies of the inner. Whenever we bring new energy from the archetypal world into our life, we encounter structures, both personal and collective, that rule us, and we must navigate carefully as the energy dismantles these patterns in order to reveal a way of being that is less conditioned. Yet this process is not easy, and too often, as in the story of the bush-digger, the inner nourishment we seek does not find its rightful place in the flow of life, where it is needed. Rather, it is misused by the ego, or diverted by the values of the collective.

We have come to the point in the story where the bush-digger and his daughter meet the King and Princess. But who is the King? Who is the Princess? The King symbolizes a patriarchal civilization, his daughter the culture of this civilization. Culture is the creative, feminine offspring of a civilization, which in a patriarchal society belongs to masculine consciousness. This is mythologically imaged by Athena, who was goddess of the arts as well as of war, springing fully armed from the head of Zeus. As we see what happens when the king and princess interact with the bush-digger and his daughter, we are seeing how the energy of the soul interacts with patriarchal civilization and its feminine offspring, its culture.

Initially there is harmony between the two pairs—it appears that the new energy easily becomes part of the established cultural patterns. We see this in the way the king and princess befriend the bush-digger and his daughter. The princess wants a playmate, and the bush-digger's daughter becomes her lady-in-waiting. At first the princess is jealous of the girl's beauty, but then becomes "fast friends" with her.

In our individual journey we often experience such initial harmony as the "honeymoon period" when the new energy released from within appears to easily fit into our life. This can even lead to an initial "high" when the inner energy is not grounded into our life, but spins off into ego fantasies.

In this story disaster lies in the friendship between the princess and the bush-digger's daughter, due to the loss of the princess's necklace. Understanding the meaning of the necklace, and why it is lost, is key to understanding the downfall of the bush-digger—why the energy of the inner does not nourish the collective.

A woman's necklace is an ancient image with two primary associations. The first is as a symbol for "diversity in unity, the beads or links being the multiplicity of manifestation, and the threads and connection the non-manifest."[12] The second association is as a symbol of a woman's individuality and worth as a person. Both associations reflect a woman's quality of relatedness. She is Psyche to a man's Eros. She is the connecting principle that brings together the different aspects of life.

But in the story, the princess takes off her necklace, symbolizing a divorce from her real feminine identity. A culture born from a patriarchal civilization will inevitably diverge from its real feminine power and understanding.

The danger of a patriarchal culture is that it too easily becomes separated from the feminine, from its roots in the unconscious where there is a rhythm in harmony with the natural world and our natural self. Our Western cultural drive to control the forces of nature, rather than working in harmony with the deep rhythm of life, has resulted in an ecological disaster. In the story of Moshkel Gosha this divorce from the natural order is reflected when the princess goes to swim. She swims, not in a natural stream, but in one "which had been made for the princess by her father." Rather than belonging to the natural flow of life of the Great Mother, the culture of a patriarchy belongs to the defined world of the Father.

Within a matriarchal society, social customs are related directly to the instinctual world of the Great Mother, as, for example, fertility rituals. Within a patriarchal society, in contrast, culture and morality often control man's instinctual drives rather than allowing them free expression. For example, the English Maypole Festival survives only as a vestige of the fertility rite it once was; the Puritans in essence suppressed it in the seventeenth century due to its orgiastic nature. The Ten Commandments, given to Moses by a patriarchal God, are probably the most famous example of a patriarchal code of morality. Such codes have a positive function in restraining and channeling instinctual forces that might otherwise overwhelm the individual and be socially destructive. But in the process often much of the wisdom and power of the feminine are lost.

Real feminine power and wisdom are vitally needed in the patriarchal civilization of the King, as well as in our contemporary culture. But the story shows us that although the feminine, in the form of the bush-digger's daughter, calls out for real nourishment, it will not be easy to bring that nourishment into the collective where it is needed. The bush-digger's daughter needs nourishment, but the stones that are given are sold by the masculine for material wealth. Thus, the inner feminine is sacrificed for worldly gain. The daughter's willingness to accept worldly goods instead of the nourishment she longs for mirrors the princess's capacity to leave her necklace on the shore of the man-made stream. Initially, the feminine is incapable of living her connection between the worlds, because she is divorced from her real being.

The feminine knows how the inner flows into the outer to nourish life. But in the story the princess swims in a man-made stream, indicating that the culture of the time is separate from the flow of life, from the inherent knowledge of how the inner and outer sustain each other. Since the culture has no established systems—personal or collective—that value the dimension of the soul, the energy of the soul crashes up against the patriarchal structures of the time, and disaster is inevitable.

Such moments of crisis are common on the individual journey as new energies begin to find their way into established patterns. For example, a seeker on a spiritual path easily becomes seduced by new powers or understandings and uses them to fill his ego's desires. Or the artist who receives the gift of his creativity from deep within sells his talent for worldly success rather than remaining true to the deeper call of his art.[13]

In our present time we have been given access to the inner world through different spiritual and psychological techniques. But how often has their use been perverted for the sake of personal gain or an ego-driven focus on our individual well-being, often disguised as "self-development"? We even use the power of the imagination and the images of the inner world as tools to manifest our own desires. Like the bush-digger, we prostitute our inner feminine and deny our world her healing and transformative potential.

But if the new energies are to find their way into the flow of life, these old ego-patterns have to break, just as the inflated world of La 'l-e Sowdagar crumbles. When the soldiers go to confiscate his palace, they find that "everything had turned to smoke and disappeared." A step has to be taken before the feminine can play her part and enable the inner world to transform the outer. We have to realize that our ego values are an inflated illusion and our power drive has to be humbled.

7
THE WISDOM OF HUMILITY

HE bush-digger's state of inflation ends with him in a dungeon, being "treated like a common criminal." Such is the humiliation suffered after a state of inflation, when the individual confronts the fact that he is but an ordinary human being. And although the bush-digger has not in fact stolen anything from the king of that country, he has stolen from another King. For the stones do not belong to him to be sold in the market place; as symbols of the Self they belong not to the ego, but to a higher realm. There in the square the bush-digger is publicly humiliated, for humility is the answer to inflation. It is humility that reminds us that we are human and not divine.

Inflation is always a danger for anyone encountering the archetypal or spiritual world. Suddenly we experience a vaster dimension than our ego-self; we feel its numinous energy, have inner experiences, or even develop extrasensory abilities. We are no longer bound by the limitations of the ordinary world, but are drawn into the world of the gods. Often the ego does not recognize that its true role is in service to the higher world; it claims the inner experience for itself and becomes identified with it. Carl Jung was very aware of this, and confronted it himself in the Siegfried dream recorded in *Memories, Dreams, Reflections*. In this dream Jung killed Siegfried, who embodied a heroic ideal which imposes itself by force of will, and it was Jung's humility that saved him from the danger of so inflated an ego:

> This identity [with Siegfried] and my heroic idealism had to be abandoned, for there are higher things than the ego's will, and to these one must bow.

Inflation is even more of a danger for those on a spiritual path, as we experience not only the archetypal world but our inner divinity. In the following extract from *Daughter of Fire*, the Sufi Master also shows how the answer to inflation is humility:

> His face was severe. He was half listening, half in Samadhi. I had the feeling

that I was boring him. He lifted his head and looked me straight in the eyes:

"Why don't you become a human being? Why don't you try to become less than the dust at my feet?" I stared at him; it seemed like an unexpected attack.

"Am I not a human being?" I was amazed and felt forlorn.

"What you are I don't know, but a human being you are not," he drawled, and it sounded like a growl. "Only when you become less than the dust at my feet will you be balanced, and only then can you be called a human being!"

C. G. Jung! flashed like lightning through my mind. In his writings, Carl Jung emphasized again and again the danger of what he calls "inflation," and our mental asylums are full of Napoleons, Cleopatras, ... not to mention even more exalted personages. I was always convinced that the process of Individuation is a preliminary step, a springboard, so to say, a starting point

to something more, which I think
would be Yoga or Self Realization.
The individuation process makes the
human being whole, complete, to be
able to take his rightful place as a balanced, perfectly normal member of the
human family. But Yoga is much more
than that. And in Yoga there must
be much more danger, consequently,
of the so-called "inflation." At one
time during the training the disciple
is bound to begin to realize his divine
origin, and then to say and to believe:
I am God! It is then that one needs
a Teacher. And the Teacher will say:
no, be careful, with those lips not yet
pure, with the heart not yet as limpid
as the Waters of Life, it is a blasphemy
to say that you are God! But a Great
Teacher does not say it so directly—he
simply teaches humility: "Become less
than the dust at my feet." How can the
inflation arise if one is made to be so
humble?[14]

In order to integrate the power and potential of the inner world, we have to recognize

our ordinary humanity. The transformative inner world does not make us more, but enables us to experience what it really means to be a human being. Without the wisdom of humility there is no balance; the ego's pride easily takes over and we create an imaginary world of which we are the lord.

Humility is often a painful lesson. The bush-digger is left in his prison cell, living off bread and water. Then, one Wednesday night, he has a dream. When we are asleep we are more open to the influence of the unconscious, and dreams have always been the easiest form of communication between the transpersonal world and ego consciousness.

In the bush-digger's dream he is approached by "a luminous holy man," dressed in green. This holy man is the archetypal figure Khidr, or the "Green One," who is linked with the ritual of *Ajil-e Moshkel Gosha*. Khidr is an archetypal figure of the direct revelation of the divine world. He tells the bush-digger that he has been inwardly blind; he has forgotten about Moshkel Gosha. This is indeed the true cause of the poor man's imprisonment. He has looked only towards the outer world, and forgotten that the source of his riches is within.

From a psychological and spiritual perspective freedom is only to be found within. To forget about the inner world is to throw away the only key that can open the prison door.

Khidr offers help to the bush-digger. Again and again the inner world tries to help us, to show us the way. The bush-digger is told, "There is a penny hidden under the door sill. Take it, buy some dried fruit, and fulfill your vow." Just as the *lapis*, the Self, is the "commonest thing," so the way to freedom lies through just one penny, symbolizing the simple wholeness of our true nature. To recognize the value of the inner self, to listen to the guidance given by dreams, does not require great wealth. Listen within for just a moment and a door can open that will change your whole life.

At the beginning of the tale, the bush-digger had to knock on his own door three times before Moshkel Gosha showed him the way. This time he has to ask three times before he is answered. The guard will not buy the dried fruit for him, nor will the man on horseback. But the old woman, whose son is dying, agrees to help him. She buys his penny's worth of fruit and agrees to share it with him and listen to his story. So once more the story of Moshkel Gosha can be told, and somebody who is in real need can be helped. Just as the bush-digger finishes telling his story, someone rushes by and shouts to the old woman that her son "has just managed to escape from the claws of Azra'il, the angel of death." If the listener is of good heart, as is the old woman, the story can reach deep into the unconscious, and bring help and healing into her life. Once again we see the transformative effect of telling this story.

For the bush-digger, once he has re-enacted the ritual of sharing the dried fruit and telling the story of Moshkel Gosha, wholeness returns to his life, for he has reconnected his individual consciousness with the Self, the archetype of wholeness. The very next morning the princess goes back to her bathing place and sees what looks like her necklace at the bottom of the stream, but "when she looked again she realized that it was a reflection of her necklace that she saw. She looked up, and there, still hanging on the branch where she had left it, was her necklace." And so the

princess discovers her mistake and on learn-
ing of it the king releases the bush-digger and
his family. The princess and the bush-digger's
daughter become friends again and in the best
fairy tale tradition, "they all lived happily ever
after." When our ordinary life is nourished
by the Self and we live in harmony with the
inner world, we are truly blessed.

8
REFLECTION
AND THE GIFT
OF CONSCIOUSNESS

EFORE we come to the end of the story, it is important to look at the symbolism of the final act that sets free the bush-digger and his wife and daughter. The princess sees the necklace reflected in the water. Reflection is an important mythic symbol, as for example in the story of Perseus, who was able to cut off the Gorgon's head by looking at her reflection in his shield. "As the word itself testifies ("reflection" means literally "bending back"), reflection is a spiritual act that runs counter to the natural process; as an act whereby we stop, call something to mind, form a picture, and take up a relation to and come to terms with what we have seen."[15]

Reflection implies consciousness. A human being's reflective powers not only separate him from the animal world, they also allow him to look into the depths of the unconscious without being assimilated back into that primal world.

At the beginning of our story the bush-digger has little consciousness. He does not know what to do with the stones and soon forgets Moshkel Gosha. As a result he unconsciously identifies with his new-found wealth and is caught by inflation. But then, due to his dream, he remembers Moshkel Gosha, who removes his difficulties through an act of reflection. Consciousness and the ability to reflect are a divine gift: "God becomes manifest in the human act of reflection."[16]

The inner world may present us with its gifts, but unless we develop the consciousness that is needed to be responsible for these gifts, their effect can be negative. Moshkel Gosha may open the doorway to the inner world, but it is for each of us to take the individual step towards greater awareness and remembrance. We cannot afford to forget the divine origin of these gifts; otherwise we are caught by hubris and imprisoned. It is particularly important when we are dealing with the inner world to reflect upon the meaning of our experience. In this way we can integrate the transformative energy and potential that come from within. Transformation is always a step towards greater consciousness and responsibility.

The story of Moshkel Gosha reflects the wonder that is within us, and how, through our need, we can be given access to this magical dimension. But the price that is asked of us is greater consciousness. If we continue in our old patterns of unconsciousness, the gifts from the inner world become negative. This is why traditionally the individual had to undergo trials and initiations before he or she was ready to be given access to the archetypal or spiritual worlds. We need to recognize that these inner gifts are not for the ego, but to be given to our neighbor whose fire has gone out, to those who are in need.

Also, it is helpful to see that the Princess's necklace was never stolen, but was there on the tree all along. We can never really be separated from our own feminine nature, as it is by definition part of our inner wholeness. It is our consciousness that changes, and comes to see that who we really are is always present.

9
A Dream About
A Good Luck Dragon

T this time in our collective history many doors to the inner worlds have been opened. Many techniques and practices that give us access to the inner are available, without our having to go through the rigors of initiations. Sadly we often use these energies for our own purpose and forget or overlook the responsibility that they place on us. We have forgotten the story of Moshkel Gosha. And yet this wisdom is all around us, and appears in unexpected ways.

The story of Moshkel Gosha is the story of anyone who has received help from within. Such help can come in many guises—a dream, a vision, or a strangely miraculous occurrence. On these occasions the door to the archetypal world opens, and its numinous and transformative power enters into the world of consciousness. And when people tell their own Moshkel Gosha stories, then, even if Moshkel Gosha is not mentioned by name, he is remembered, and is thus able to continue his work: to help those who are in real need to find their way.

My tale of Moshkel Gosha is in the form of a dream I had the night after I finished working on the above commentary. It is a dream which both removed personal difficulties and illustrates one of the central themes of the bush-digger's tale.

> I am invited to a party by a friend of mine who is very wealthy, and in this party there is a dragon ceremony. I am told by all the people there that the dragon is covered with money and one should try to take as much money off the dragon as possible. When the dragon enters it is a long dragon made of gold paper, on which are stuck a number of gold-colored one-pound coins. This dragon is a "Good Luck" dragon. I take two of the one-pound coins, and although I see there are more coins I feel that two are enough.
>
> At this moment the man whose party it is says that you shouldn't take any money from the dragon. In fact, he says, the money is only put on the dragon because people would get upset otherwise.

I then ask this man: "Why does everybody say that you should take money from the dragon if that isn't the thing to do?" It seemed very significant that no one had ever asked this question before.

The answer was, "Because people don't believe in dragons anymore."

The right attitude to have towards the dragon is just to let the dragon work. I looked at the dragon; it had the most wonderful green eyes.

A dragon is an ancient symbol for the tremendous power and transformative energy of the inner world. A dragon does not just belong to the personal psyche, but also to the collective. A dragon ceremony is a traditional way to integrate this power, so that the dragon energy can benefit life. But in today's ceremony there is no reverence for the dragon. Rather the attitude is to "try to take as much money off the dragon as possible." Our Western attitude of greed and disrespect for our inner and outer nature has corrupted the ancient ways through which the power of the inner world can nourish us.

Moshkel Gosha

In the dream I am told that in fact one should not take money from the dragon, that "money is only put on the dragon because people would get upset otherwise." Our culture has so little understanding of the ways of the inner world that we can only appreciate the images of our own greed: we only see the natural world for what it can give us, the energy that we can take from it. We know this only too well in the ravages of our industrial world. We do not appreciate how this greed has affected the inner world, which we also approach with eyes of greed. How often do we use a spiritual or psychological practice with the attitude of "what can it give me?" or "how will I benefit?" We do not appreciate the real nature of the inner world, which is not just concerned with our personal gain.

Just as the natural physical world is not here just for the benefit of humanity, neither is the archetypal world of the dragon. We are all a part of a greater whole that has a purpose far beyond our understanding. We need to become conscious of this greater dimension so that we can have the correct attitude of reverence to the wonders of the inner and outer world. In the dream it is significant that I ask the question, "Why does everybody say that you should take money from the dragon if that isn't the thing to do?" Asking the question is always an act of consciousness, as in the grail legend when Parsival has to ask the question, "For whom serves the grail?" The answer, "The grail serves the grail king," makes the individual aware of the transcendent nature of his quest: he is no longer caught in the grip of the ego.

In my dream I was told the sad truth: "People don't believe in dragons anymore." How can we work with the transformative nature of the inner world when we no longer believe in it? If we only believe in the goals of the ego, how can we respect the larger dimension of the archetypes and the Self? How can we appreciate the wisdom of this inner world, the ancient knowledge of dragons?

The correct approach to the images of the unconscious is just to let them work. One does not "do" anything with them, but in allowing them to be, giving them a place in our house, in our life, we allow their dynamic energy to have its effect. In this dream the dragon is a "Good Luck" dragon, and so, like Moshkel Gosha, its energy will resolve difficulties and bring good fortune. And the color of the dragon's eyes is very auspicious, for not only is green the color of growth and becoming, but it is also the color of Khidr, the Sufi archetypal figure of inner transformation and the divine revelation.

In the story of the bush-digger, he does not know what to do with the stones. He does not realize that just leaving them in the corner of his house is enough, that their energy alone will transform his life and benefit his neighbors. Forgetting Moshkel Gosha, he sells the stones for money. In my dream people no longer believe in dragons, and not knowing what to do with a "Good Luck" dragon, they just take money from it. In both cases the real transformative potential of the inner world is denied.

But if we can remember our own inner heritage, listen to its wisdom, and allow its energy into our life, we will find that many of our difficulties are resolved. The archetypal world is not limited by the conditioning of our ego. It has resources far beyond our limited perspective. But just as the dragon needs to be believed in, so does Moshkel Gosha need to be remembered. Through telling the story of Moshkel Gosha we reconnect with this inner reality. Then its healing and transformative power can become present in our lives.

10
A SOUTH AMERICAN STORY OF MOSHKEL GOSHA

OSHKEL Gosha appears in unexpected places and helps in unexpected ways. A South American friend told me the following story which happened to her:

"One summer I was staying in a hotel in central New York. My husband and I walked to a local restaurant for an evening meal, but as I sat down to eat I realized that I had lost an emerald earring. It was very valuable, and more important it had belonged to my mother-in-law and was a gift from her. We went back along the street to the hotel and searched everywhere. It was just getting dark and so we borrowed some torches from the hotel. Just as I was despairing of ever finding the earring, I remembered a story I had been told as a child:

There was once a bandit who robbed from the people and did many terrible deeds. However, just before he died he repented of everything he had done. When he died he stood before the Virgin Mary, who said to him, "Although you repented, you did so many terrible things that I cannot allow you into paradise. You will have to go to purgatory. But I will let you help people by finding things for them. And then they will have masses said for you, and slowly you will be able to pay your debts and go to paradise."

"When I remembered this story I asked the former bandit to help me find the earring. I said that if I found it I would buy him $100 worth of masses. A moment later, I looked under some litter, and to my joy, discovered my earring. The next day I kept my vow and went to the local Catholic church. I asked a young priest how much it cost to have a mass said for someone. He said $5. So I told him the story and asked him to say 20 masses for this old Spanish bandit. He looked at me as if I was crazy, but he took the $100."

Moshkel Gosha is an archetypal story that appears in many different forms. At the core of all these stories is the same simple truth: through remembering the archetypal world we allow its transpersonal dimension to bring its magical qualities into our lives.

BIBLIOGRAPHY

Bennett, J. G. *The Masters of Wisdom*. London: Turnstone, 1977.

Circlot, J. E. *A Dictionary of Symbols*. London: Routledge and Kegan Paul, 1962.

Cooper, J. C. *An Illustrated Encyclopedia of Traditional Symbols*. London: Thames and Hudson, 1978.

Corbin, Henry. *Creative Imagination in the Sufism of Ibn 'Arabi*. Princeton: Princeton University Press, 1969.

—."Mundus Imaginalis." Spring, 1977, pp. 1-19.

Eliot, T. S. *Four Quartets*. London: Faber and Faber, 1944.

Hall, Nor. *The Moon and the Virgin*. New York: Harper and Row, 1980.

Jung, C. G. *Collected Works*. London: Routledge and Kegan Paul.

—.*Memories, Dreams, Reflections*. London: Flamingo, 1983.

Lao Tzu. *Tao Te Ching*. Trans. Gia-Fu Feng and Jane English. Aldershot: Wildwood House, 1973.

Luke, Helen. *The Inner Story*. New York: Crossroad Publishing Co., 1982.

Shah, Idries. *Caravan of Dreams*. London: Octagon Press, 1968.

Shushud, Hasan. *The Masters of Wisdom of Central Asia*. Ellingstring UK: Coombe Springs Press, 1983.

Tweedie, Irina. *Daughter of Fire: A Diary of a Spiritual Training with a Sufi Master*. Inverness: Golden Sufi Center, 1986.

Whitmont, Edward. *The Symbolic Quest*. Princeton: Princeton University Press, 1978.

Notes

1. J. G. Bennett, *The Masters of Wisdom*, p. 159, and Hasan Shushud, *The Masters of Wisdom of Central Asia*, p. 33.
2. Irina Tweedie, *Daughter of Fire*. p. 148.
3. J. E. Cirlot, *A Dictionary of Symbols*, p. 79.
4. Atharva Veda, 10.8.11., quoted by C. G. Jung, *Collected Works* (hereafter referred to as C. W.), vol. 6, para 329.
5. Recently, the term "Moshkel Gosha" has found a far more mundane application in colloquial usage. It is employed when one comes up against some official or bureaucratic obstacle which cannot be gotten around unless one has either influence or money. In the absence of influence, one rubs the thumb against the index finger, and says "Moshkel Gosha"—in other words implying that bribery is available.
6. Khidr, or the "Green One," is a central archetypal Sufi figure. He is associated with the direct revelation of the divine world. He drank the water of life and thereby became immortal. The color green is said by the Sufi to be the color of the realization of God.
7. Irina Tweedie, *Daughter of Fire*, p. 326.
8. The story of the birth of Christ—born in a barn, in a cow manger—can be read as imaging the same psychological fact, with the Christ child as a symbol for the Self.
9. C. G. Jung, C.W. vol. 12, para 103.

10. A real-life example of the ego's becoming identified with an archetype is Marilyn Monroe. She may be best understood as someone invaded, indeed possessed, by the archetype of the goddess of love, Aphrodite. The world related to Marilyn in an archetypal way. Without awareness of the mythological label of "Aphrodite," America simply regarded her as its sex symbol and as a love goddess. However, the tragedy of Marilyn Monroe was that she was so possessed by the power of this archetype, and inflated by it, that she was unable to find meaning in her personal life. "Embodying Aphrodite, how could she be expected to see men in any position other than prone, in adoration?" (E. Whitmont, *The Symbolic Quest*, p. 100.) And so, unfulfilled by personal relationships, she passed from "one sordid affair into another, and ... finally to suicide."

11. C. G. Jung, *Memories, Dreams, Reflections*, p. 218.

12. Nor Hall, *The Moon and the Virgin*, p. 163.

13. F. Scott Fitzgerald is an example of this. In his own work he acknowledges this tragedy.

14. Irina Tweedie, *Daughter of Fire*, p. 378.

15. C. G. Jung, C.W. vol. 11, para. 235n.

16. C. G. Jung, C.W. vol. 11, para. 238.

ABOUT the AUTHOR

LLEWELLYN VAUGHAN-LEE, Ph.D., is a Sufi teacher in the Naqshbandiyya-Mujaddidiyya Sufi Order. Born in London in 1953, he has followed the Naqshbandi Sufi path since he was nineteen. In 1991 he moved to Northern California and founded The Golden Sufi Center (goldensufi.org).

He has authored a series of books that give a detailed exploration of the stages of spiritual and psychological transformation experienced on the Sufi path, with a particular focus on the use of dreamwork as inner guidance on the journey. Since 2000 the focus of his writing and teaching has been on spiritual responsibility in our present time of transition, the awakening global consciousness of oneness, and spiritual ecology (workingwithoneness.org). He has also been featured in the TV series *Global Spirit* and was interviewed by Oprah Winfrey as a part of her *Super Soul Sunday* series.

ABOUT the PUBLISHER

THE GOLDEN SUFI CENTER is a California Religious Non-Profit Corporation dedicated to making the teachings of the Naqshbandi Sufi path available to all seekers. For further information about the activities and publications, please contact:

THE GOLDEN SUFI CENTER
P.O. Box 456
Point Reyes Station, CA 94956-0456
www.goldensufi.org

ADDITIONAL PUBLICATIONS
from THE GOLDEN SUFI CENTER

by **IRINA TWEEDIE**

DAUGHTER OF FIRE:
A Diary of a Spiritual Training with a Sufi Master

by **LLEWELLYN VAUGHAN-LEE**

SPIRITUAL ECOLOGY:
10 Practices to Reawaken the Sacred in Everyday Life

FOR LOVE OF THE REAL:
A Story of Life's Mystical Secret

WITHIN THE HEART OF HEARTS:
A Story of Mystical Love

SPIRITUAL ECOLOGY:
The Cry of the Earth

DARKENING OF THE LIGHT:
Witnessing the End of an Era

PRAYER OF THE HEART
IN CHRISTIAN & SUFI MYSTICISM

FRAGMENTS OF A LOVE STORY:
Reflections on the Life of a Mystic

THE RETURN OF THE FEMININE & THE WORLD SOUL

ALCHEMY OF LIGHT:
Working with the Primal Energies of Life